the bl

First published 2019 by The Hedgehog Poetry Press
Published in the UK by
The Hedgehog Poetry Press
5, Coppack House
Churchill Avenue
Clevedon
BS21 6QW
www.hedgehogpress.co.uk

ISBN: 978-1-9160908-4-2

9 8 7 6 5 4 3 2 1
A CIP Catalogue record for this book is available from the British Library.

the blue hour

by

Mick Yates

the blue hour is a period of morning and evening twilight

when the sun is below the horizon

colouring the sky a deep blue

for my very dear friend
Annette Snowdon
come sit with me awhile
and read these scattered words on paper
then return to your own world once more
i shall never forget our first meeting
and will keep you always in my heart

Contents

the blue hour

a fragile boundary
that separates night and day
and the living from the dead
a prussian blue haze
between what lies unspoken
and what was once said
the fragrant remembrance
of earlier happy days
the lingering kiss the last dance
the subtle smiles of new romance
all these fond memories and more
now gathering dust behind a closed door
blurring the threshold between present and past
the passing of sad sweet things
that are doomed never to last
these dear remembered yearnings
for times now long lost
the painful truth the bitter cost

transcendence

once upon a time
on a long lost day in childhood
on a bike ride in the country
where a golden sun shines high
in the azure blue sky
resting beside a silver stream
stealing a few still moments from time
while the world ceases turning
and hangs by a silver thread
from the roof of the universe
in a trance or maybe in a dream
it happened to me once back then
though has never since returned again

old friends

we should regard them all
as our favourite toys from childhood
the special presents gifted to you in life
the ones you could never
quite throw away as you got older
the ones that still felt good
still felt comfortable to have around
the trouble is that even toys
grow a little ragged with advancing age
the fabric of the teddy bear wears thin
the dress on the doll becomes tattered
the colours fade slowly over time
the stitching comes undone
they become threadbare and transparent
yet still you cannot discard them from your life
for they are such an important part of you
it seems some things in this world
we just do not want to disappear forever

long meg and her daughters

what enchantment is this?
what secret sorcery?
what magic and mystery
is abroad in the air this evening
around the ancient stone circle
this summer solstice in cumbria?
the standing stones lean forward
as if they have a secret to tell
to anyone who cares to listen
it is one we believed in once
when the world revolved
on a simpler axis in time and space
it was a communal sense a common good
a belief we all shared and understood
in this sacred place many years ago
but have now long since forgotten

the common sense

it would not do for human kind
to be too similar to each other
it is our differences that we should celebrate
it is those very human qualities good or bad
that make us unique as individuals
as societies as countries and as nations
together we are capable of both greatness and failure
the decision is ours collectively to take
we may wage wars against each other
yet we have set foot upon the moon
we have journeyed common paths together
since life on this planet began
we are not simply woman or man
mother father daughter or son
we are bound together in this as one
but as time is slowly running out
a far better future beckons us both here and elsewhere
so let us unite in our differences
and embrace our common futures together

immigrants

it is not a good place to be
dwelling on the fringes of humanity
as outsiders from the security of the pack
they are well aware of the protection they lack
of the things that are said behind their back
they feel different from all the others
forever solitary amongst their sisters and brothers
they are constantly vulnerable
the most prone to vicious attack
of all the most needy and deserving people in the world
they too often find themselves alone
they are made to feel the most unwelcome
by a small and ignorant minority of those
in whose country they seek to find a home
sadly instead of open arms
they find only closed minds

ephemera

did you ever
make sandcastles as a child
on the endless blue hot sunny days
in the long lost summers of childhood
when the tide was far out to sea?
digging deep channels for the moat
building high turrets from buckets
filled to the brim with still damp sand?
remember how impenetrable they seemed?
how firm and solid you constructed them?
then waiting for the tide to return
so confident in your building skills
so defiant in the strength of your architecture?
like the sandcastles you built way back then
nothing in this life is permanent

empathy

ellen first got really ill
maybe six months ago
it was uncertain even then
whether she would make it
through the many operations
then she got better
it was a great summer here
they enjoyed barbecues and wine
had themselves a really good time
then in early august
the sickness came back again
and she had to undergo
more operations more pain
her husband is beside himself
i try my best for him
but still can't explain
what i feel for them
the sorrow and the pain
the inevitable loss
the non-existent gain

endgame

ellen is outside in the garden
on one of the last days of summer
hanging out the washing to dry
tidying the plants removing the fading flowers
she and her husband potted earlier in the year
the prognosis is not good for her however
in two days she returns to hospital
for a final operation to cure her illness
although both she and her consultant
know that it will not restore her health
the outcome has now become inevitable
i feel a deep sadness and desperation
that she will not live to see
the seasons turn again next year
the brevity the cruelty the sheer brutality
of life is completely beyond my comprehension
i sat with her husband holding hands yesterday
we talked very little there was nothing left to say

renaissance

dawn opened her sleepy eyes
somewhere way over in the east
in a place i did not recognise
and had never been before
i sat silent and watched
as the first rays touched my skin
and warmth flowed through my body
still cold from the passing night
a new day stretched before me
full of strange untrodden futures
in the slowly growing light
a distant river turned to molten gold
so full of hope and promise
and the possibility of flight

a storm in slovakia

there is something brewing in the air
it has been lurking there
all the torrid day long
something unspoken something wrong
the signs have been ominous
the temperature rising unbearably
the pressure building slowly
to an inevitable breaking point
they sit enclosed in the log cabin
as two strangers in a foreign land
waiting for some kind of catharsis
and now that it has finally arrived
they each give thanks separately and silently
for the thunder the lightning the vicious tempest
but when it does all finally blow away
as strangers in a log cabin they will still always remain
with little to say to each other
except mumbled inconsequential comments
about the weather and the rain
about the deep sadness of it all
the absolution and the pain

st martin's cathedral – bratislava

i had not intended to cry that day
after all i was on holiday
it was hot and i needed shade
so i walked inside
seeking release from the sun
sitting silently in the calm interior
my mind was fixed on laughter
and the celebration of life
an old woman genuflected before the altar
sat down in a pew in front of me
she was lost in deep thought
after some moments the first tear came
then others followed rapidly
as her memories came back to her
she dabbed her eyes with a handkerchief
as i too shed tears for her sorrows

conversations with vincent

it is a rather dull day
outside the summerhouse in my garden
he sits closely beside me
as we enjoy afternoon tea
he tells me how last summer
he first began to paint sunflowers
how he so adored their brilliance
how for him they represented life and hope
how it was a motif he would return to again
how they helped him cope
with the bad days when they came
how he preferred bright colours
to the blackness of despair

dear whoever

if i were you
i would be very wary
of ever giving advice to anyone
it has a nasty habit of backfiring
of exploding in your face
like un-pricked sausages
sizzling in a hot frying pan
far better to remain impartial
to keep your own counsel
and to fend off any such requests
with a polite but firm refusal
far better in my limited experience
to let your actions in life
do the talking rather than your voice
and most certainly pay no attention whatsoever
to what i have just written to you
better to learn your own lessons in life
that would be my best advice

aftermath

you can tell by the density of the flow
that the river means serious business this time
a vast bulk of rolling angry water
a slow motion shouldering of rain
as if a gigantic tin of black treacle
has been dropped on the kitchen floor of our town
it is an organic living sculpture
evolving through time and passage
into a seething herd of wild horses
galloping madly through the lives of mortals
leaving a crescendo of human misery in its wake
a brutal testimony to the legacy of storm desmond

appleby horse fair

skidding wildly down the slippery ramp
young gypsy lads and lasses ride bareback
on their glistening feral mounts
into the baptismal waters of the river eden
these aspiring romany guardians of the genus equus
these water gods and nymphs of this tribal gathering
these natural spiritual acolytes in this ancient ritual
arrogantly parade their pride and expertise
before an admiring audience of onlookers
all deeply envious of their youth their lifestyle
and the sheer wild hedonism of their existence

metamorphosis

the electricity pylons
look like dormant triffids tonight
maybe when we have gone to bed
they will rise and spring into life
walk through the wild pasture
at the back of our log cabin
and stroll down to the town
for a late beer or two
or maybe even a night on the tiles
returning in the early morning
to their normal static state
as if nothing unusual had happened
and the life of pylons
has always been conducted this way

vernal equinox

orion is a majestic sight
proudly defined against the lampblack sky
in the frosty air of a late march night
a regal presence in the firmament
commanding respect from the changing seasons
ushering us onwards into the future
trailing us in her shimmering wake
urging us into the potent promise of spring

birdsong

it is late evening in late may
under a most unseasonable grey sky
two blackbirds or thrushes
hold a conversation from rooftop to tree
they are indistinguishable as either species
one because it cannot be seen
the other because it exists in silhouette
against the drab grey sky
is it courtship?
is it wooing?
who can say for the conversation
ends abruptly from the one to the other
who ended it first?
the male or the female?
and either way if so then why?
it is hard to say for certain
for one exists in silhouette
against the drab grey sky
and the other is invisible in a tree

a peculiar dislocation

so here we are
gathered on a sunny evening in june
i am surrounded by family and friends
for a celebratory meal and laughter
it is time to give thanks
for our communal good fortune
a time to relax and enjoy life
a sudden freeze-frame descends from the sky
holding me static in time and place
i sit alone as if removed from reality
from what i see and know and love
a stranger among familiar faces
an alien in my own land
the words i hear spoken are in another language
one i no longer seem to understand
tell me exactly someone for what purpose i am here?
tell me exactly someone who am i anymore?

flight path

swallows seagulls and rooks
are criss-crossing the skies this morning
like planes arriving and leaving
from london heathrow airport
i have never seen or heard
of birds colliding in the air
so how do they navigate so accurately
on short hops and long haul journeys?
do they have air traffic controllers
operating from control towers hidden in the trees?
or is it some inherent instinct within
that gives them such majesty in flight?

spider war

there is a spider
of unknown genus or species
that lives behind the glass
in the wing mirror of our car
at this time of the year in june
and for many years past
either this or another spider
weaves dense intricate webs overnight
for me to discover in the morning
i should not do it i know
but i destroy these webs every day
with either my fingers or water
i do not want to destroy its impressive endeavour
or the means by which it captures its food
but if left unchecked the spider would cover our car
in an intricate net of its own design
is this something i should allow?
we go away on holiday for a fortnight soon
i wonder what it will have done on our return
and whether i shall ever find our car again

innocence

the brownie meeting
is over for the night
the pack is dispersing
the girl scouts are coming out
and all is laughter and delight
such simple pleasures
they find in shared games
in common interests
and the company of friends
when these days of innocence
find their natural ends
what is there to replace them?
what is there that as adults we lack
and can never ever quite get back?

romance

there is another love
that makes no grand declarations
of intent anymore
that needs no expensive presents
to sustain its existence
this other love is exquisitely rare
takes time to grow to mature to care
and smiles in silent adoration
for this is a love that endures
that relishes the shared passion of solitude
that savours the occasional bottle of wine
and the melodic murmurs of muted music
for this is a love that intuitively understands
the secret coded messages there
the intimacy and mystique of sensual stares
the gentle holding of hands
before retiring eagerly upstairs

mortality

i stumble i mumble i bumble
i cannot remember who i am anymore
did i ever know myself?
were we ever formally introduced?
and if so on what occasion?
and was this how the conversation went?
' good evening sir so pleased to meet you
  i am you and you are i
  we are identical twins forever inseparable
  for all eternity'
i wait i wait i wait
like the dying embers in the grate
but for what i enquire?
for the last of the living fire
what is that knock on the door?
are we locked up and secure?
i don't know anymore
but when will it come?
when will it come?

sometime after dawn
before the setting of the sun

memories

they will be few in number sometimes
sparse in recollection
like an archaeological site
barren and dusty
in the hot summer sun
hard clay difficult to breach
with a shovel and trowel
the finds hard earned
caked in the dense soil of prehistory
the students idle and complaining
the climate humid and draining
the occasional rumble of thunder
the periodic raining

a photograph album

it was a birthday present for me
bought from a second-hand store
or an antiques shop somewhere
old black and white photographs
of lake ullswater in the lake district
beautiful ageing snapshots frozen in time
all except the last one curiously
an image of the cenotaph in london
at a remembrance day service held long ago
shortly after the first world war possibly
an image so out of context
so incongruous within the collection
an image that spoke of another memory
an image that told another story
one of personal sadness
one of lost love maybe?

moral dilemma

outside it is twilight
inside the kitchen however
a weary fly batters itself senseless
against the firmly closed window
in a desperate bid for freedom
it has been inside all day
sneaking in like a burglar
looking for food to steal
when the window was wide open
to let in the early morning air
it has feasted on stale cat food all day since then
and now that its appetite is satisfied
it seeks once more the sky outside
vulnerable and weak now though
to open the window and let it go
would be a kindness perhaps
were it not for the circling bats outside
beyond the kitchen door
who would find it easy prey
what does one do for the best therefore
at this the end of the day?

existentialism

the older i become
the less i understand of this absurd world
for me to even consider our illogical place
in an apparently meaningless universe
serves only to emphasise my complete lack of understanding
of concepts way beyond my comprehension
that poet t s eliot almost got it right
when he spoke of birth copulation and death
he should have mentioned also however
the beneficial effects of alcohol and drugs
both useful antidotes to our universal angst
in my humble unphilosophical opinion

r s v p

youth youth
knocking at the door as ever
asking questions i still can't answer
i so admire your strut your arrogant posture
i so admire your certainty your absolute conviction
i so covet your eternal optimism
and your sense of purpose
i wish you well my adventurers
may you find the answers
i am still searching for
and if you do solve the riddle somehow
please let me know
yours sincerely etc.

halloween

the odd remaining leaf
lets go and falls silently
to lie on the ground
joining others too weary
with the onset of winter
to offer any effective resistance
the clouds are discarded feathers
dropped from the wings of migrant birds
and only the sky burns
molten magenta in defiance

legacy

too many friends have departed recently
lost forever somewhere in the cosmos
thoughtlessly leaving me alone in this world
they were not mere acquaintances
but those of far greater significance
who have imprinted themselves deeply
in my heart and in my soul
what do i do now that they are gone?
do i ponder the injustice of mortality?
or wait patiently for them to call me home?

eternal

the night sky
is still there
as it ever was
still black
still endless
still sprinkled
with a myriad
of silver stars
indifferent to humanity
as it ever will be

for my daughters and their daughters

what can i write about you
my special and unique girls
that has not been written before?
there are so few words
i can grasp to depict my pride
in you and your achievements
for you are your own creations
i may have given you
the base clay with which to work
but you moulded yourselves
into your own individual images
as in legend pygmalion created galatea
i merely took the seedlings of your lives
planted them and nurtured them
and watched the beautiful flowers grow

minor miracles

so many people believe in them
so many people spend their lives
visiting shrines churches and temples
trying to discover one for themselves
others wander the world restlessly
in the belief that such a find
might somehow change their lives forever
maybe it is the small things in life
that matter most in reality?
the mundane events that we often ignore completely
most of the time in our everyday lives?
is it not sufficient enough really
to be able to hold the hand
of someone you love dearly?

first love

when i was sixteen
she took me walking
on the mountains in the lake district
we rested on a summit one day
lying on our backs in the sun
she taught me to watch the clouds
to see shapes faces and visions
in them as they floated past
she told me most things in life do not last
like our youthful summer love
and even life itself
now many years later
i still search the clouds for reasons
still see her face there and wonder

one night

one night
unable to sleep
i woke in the early hours of morning
i watched you in your peaceful slumber
your beautiful hair
cascading like a waterfall
tumbling in its splendour
your eyes closed
and full of secret dreams
one night
unable to sleep
i woke in the early hours of morning
in silent adoration of your beauty

lost and found

everything that was lost
has now been found again
with the passage of time
where there was once only a past
there is now a future
and the promise of new beginnings
the ghosts still remain of course
we keep in regular contact
they remind me every day
that the present is all we have
that in each moment lasts forever

silloth

the scots pines lean eastward
buffeted as they are by westerly winds
tearing across the wide tidal estuary
this once vibrant seaside resort
now wears a veil of fading grandeur
as it has done so since
the demise of its long lost railway
these days only random determined visitors
come to this once popular place
and the promenades and parks
seem wistful in their emptiness
the seagulls still cry out loudly
across the vast solway firth
a haunting sound mournful and lost

traveller's grave

there is not much to distinguish this final resting place
a scattering of rocks under a single yew tree
are all that remain of a life now long gone
look carefully though and you will see
two plastic roses and a teddy bear
worn thin with age and the elements
the trinkets and mementos of a short life
measured in months not years
listen carefully though and you will hear
the cry of a red kite circling overhead
and the gentle sigh of a child's last breath
floating down the nearby river ithon on its final journey

(St. Cewydd's Church, Disserth, Powys, Mid-Wales 1996)